Sustainable Buildings
The Client's Role

Joanna Eley

RIBA  **Publishing**

© RIBA Enterprises Ltd., 2011

Published by RIBA Publishing, 15 Bonhill Street, London EC2P 2EA

ISBN 978 1 85946 366 6

Stock code 74295

The right of Joanna Eley to be identified as the Author of this Work has been asserted in accordance with the Copyright, Design and Patents Act 1988

British Library Cataloguing in Publications Data
A catalogue record for this book is available from the British Library.

Commissioning Editor: Lucy Harbor
Project Editor: Gray Publishing
Designed and typeset by Gray Publishing, Tunbridge Wells
Printed and bound by Polestar Wheatons

While every effort has been made to check the accuracy and quality of the information given in this publication, neither the Author nor the Publisher accept any responsibility for the subsequent use of this information, for any errors or omissions that it may contain, or for any misunderstandings arising from it. All parties must rely exclusively upon their own skill and judgement or upon their advisers when using this publication and RIBA Enterprises Ltd. assumes no liability to any user or any third party.

RIBA Publishing is part of RIBA Enterprises Ltd.

www.ribaenterprises.com

Contents

Foreword

There is an overwhelming scientific consensus that climate change is taking place as a consequence of greenhouse gas (GHG) emissions from human activity. Global temperatures are rising because of the increasing concentration of carbon dioxide in our atmosphere. This is why in July 2009, the leaders of the European Union and the G8 announced an objective to reduce GHG emissions by at least 80% below 1990 levels by 2050.

The UK's commitment to reduce carbon dioxide and other GHG emissions is now a matter of legal obligation. Responsible for 40–60% of the UK's GHG emissions, the construction industry is entering a period of transformation, and low-carbon design will play an increasingly important role. Legislation will mitigate the effects of carbon emissions, with the British government setting a zero-carbon target by 2016 for new homes and 2019 for non-domestic buildings.

The role of the client is pivotal in achieving sustainable low-carbon development, leading by example to set a vision for good design that minimises our impact on the environment.

At project inception, the client is able to shape the brief, ensure collaboration within the team and define balanced, informed, sustainable objectives.

In recognising the complexity of the topic area, the RIBA Sustainable Futures Group helped define the scope for this guide, which covers sustainable development, mitigation, financial incentive and penalties, resilience, adaptation, measurement, building handover and post-occupancy evaluation. It provides a road map to sustainable development through the layers of legislation, accreditation and targets, identifying opportunities for the client to ensure the building, space or place contributes positively to our environment.

Alan Shingler
Chair of RIBA Sustainable Futures

About the guide

This guide is for you, a client wishing to have a sustainable building. It will help you to make the best use of available professional advice and knowledge. It will make it easier for you to understand the choices and to communicate your vision to your design team. Along the way, the guide outlines why sustainability matters in building projects, how it can serve your own and wider objectives and, most importantly, your essential role in achieving it.

Regardless of how experienced you are or what *kind* of sustainable building you're hoping to build – a refurbishment, a major remodelling or a new build – the principles set out here will help you to get your project off on the right footing and see you through to a building that meets your brief.

The guide is structured in two main parts: Part 1 explains what you need to understand about current legislation and targets that will affect your project. Part 2 alerts you to what you need to consider at each stage.

Part 1

Introduction

As the client who wants a sustainable building, you are in the best position to give the whole project the leadership it needs to bring this about. Of course, your project must meet minimum standards to comply with building legislation, planning requirements and achieve wider government targets. However, to deliver real sustainable benefits, you will have to go beyond these minimum standards and it is by doing this that other tangible rewards are brought about. Positive effects include:

- Keeping down operating costs over the life of your building.
- Increasing the value of your building because users and potential buyers/renters will appreciate the low costs in use.
- Providing a safer, healthier environment for users by considering their well-being, reducing pollution and providing for affordable comfort.

What you do as the client has an important impact on the success of your project. This guide includes a series of checklists highlighting the actions that are most likely to improve the sustainability of your project, all underpinned by some general principles:

- **Consider all options before finalising your project aims.** You might not need a new building; altering the one you have now, moving into a different existing one or doing without a building entirely might be a more sustainable, better solution.
- **Visit exemplar buildings.** Talk to their designers and users about actual energy performance in use, and find out whether the building is easy to manage and a pleasure to use.
- **Set targets for reducing running costs.** Understand the costs of running your current building, especially the amount of energy you use, by taking expert advice. This will help you to set targets for reductions in costs in your new project.
- **Put a value on your targets for sustainability.** Doing so will help you to understand the relative importance to you of what you plan for your new building.

What is sustainability?

The United Nations definition of sustainability is the reconciliation of environmental, social and economic demands – the 'three pillars' of sustainability – for the immediate and future well-being of individuals and communities (see Figure 1). Although buildings play social and economic roles in accommodating families, community services and workplaces, this guide concentrates mostly on the benefits of pursuing the environmental agenda.

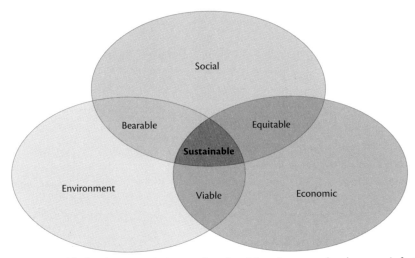

Figure 1: Sustainable development: the interaction of social, environmental and economic factors. Source: based on Adams, W.M. (2006).

Sustainability in relation to buildings involves limiting their unwanted impacts on the environment and subsumes many technical concepts. For example, 'green' or 'ecological' sustainability emphasises the need to protect biodiversity and natural cycles of plants, animals and water from developments. 'Environmental' sustainability has similar connotations but addresses the needs of people more overtly. 'Low- or zero-carbon development' is a way to limit the damaging climate changing effects (see later) ascribed to the release of carbon dioxide (CO_2) into the atmosphere and is closely associated with limiting energy use. These and some other terms are often used interchangeably and are all implied in this guide when referring to 'sustainable buildings'.

To echo the widely quoted definition of sustainability in the influential Brundtland Report (1987), sustainable buildings should and can create places that meet 'the needs of the present without compromising the ability of future generations to meet their own needs'. In practice, this means that during building design and construction you should commit to:

- Minimise use of resources – energy, water, materials, especially non-renewable resources.
- Minimise unwanted outputs – greenhouse gases (GHGs) such as CO_2, pollution and other wastes.
- Maximise the health and well-being benefits for users and the local community.

Buildings and climate change

There is a broad consensus that the world's climate is changing in undesirable ways because of the release of GHGs such as CO_2 from human activity. These result in trends in the UK towards:

- increased average temperatures
- reduced summer and increased winter rainfall averages
- more violent extremes of temperature and rainfall
- storms with greater wind forces
- rising sea levels
- more frequent coastal and river flooding and urban flash floods.

In construction and use, buildings account for a substantial proportion of the total release of CO_2. Their design, the materials they are made of, the way they are built, fitted out and used shape our lives, influence how we use energy, water and other scarce resources, create pollution and waste and affect our health and well-being. Despite wide recognition of these impacts, many buildings still:

- fail to meet their design targets for energy use and comfort
- prove too complicated to operate as intended
- miss opportunities to support responsible use of resources
- generate unnecessary waste and pollution, in particular CO_2, in use
- cannot be efficiently recycled at the end of their useful lives.

The RIBA has published a set of eight free-of-charge documents, their 'Climate Change Toolkits', which cover basic principles and technical information, with links and introductions to the latest guidance. Although designed for architects, they contain background information that you will find useful.[1]

---

1   www.architecture.com/FindOutAbout/Sustainabilityandclimatechange/ClimateChange/Toolkits.aspx

---

Buildings have a large impact on the environment[2]

- According to the United Nations Environment Programme, buildings consume between 30–40% of global energy. There is no single larger global contributor – and thereby potential reducer – of carbon than the building sector.
- Buildings account for 40–60% of the energy consumed in Britain and generate 50% of UK carbon emissions.
- Green buildings can reduce CO_2 emissions by more than 35% – and in some cases can be carbon neutral.
- Green buildings also reduce waste output by 70%, water usage by 40% and energy usage between 30–50% – in some cases producing energy that can be sent back to the grid.
- The building sector directly employs 5–10% of the workforce in most countries.

Tackling climate change: mitigation and adaptation

Two strategies are used to combat climate change: mitigation and adaptation. Mitigation focuses on minimising the generation of GHGs. Adaptation is about responding to anticipated change.

Building layouts, materials and technological norms have evolved to allow us to make buildings that protect us from familiar weather patterns. New and existing buildings, and the exterior spaces around them, must adapt to meet future changes in the climate. What used to work no longer necessarily holds good.

Climate projections

The Department for Environment, Food and Rural Affairs (Defra) published its most recent climate change projections in 2009, updating its earlier 2002 predictions (Defra, 2009). Defra uses a variety of data sources to model, for three different carbon emissions scenarios (high, medium and low), what climate changes can be expected in different areas of the UK. Designers should consult this information to help decide what should be taken into account. The immediate and secondary consequences of changes in, for example, temperature, rainfall averages and extremes are discussed.

---

2   Sources: Energy Saving Trust, www.energysavingtrust.org.uk; UKGBC, www.ukgbc.org; United Nations Environment Programme, 2007, *Buildings and Climate Change.*

The economic context

Sustainable design need not cost more

Sustainable buildings need not cost significantly more to build than any other and will be cheaper to run. This is especially true if the critical issues are addressed early enough to be resolved through design. Bolt-on solutions, i.e. ones added after most design decisions have been made, become increasingly expensive and ineffective the further into the project they are introduced. Research indicates that initial capital cost typically increases by between 3–5% for a sustainable building (Davis Langdon, 2007).

Working out lifetime costs

Lifecycle costing (as it is known) is a straightforward way to help you to predict the future cost of running your building. The lifetime cost is made up of a mixture of regular maintenance, repairs, replacement of elements that have a shorter life than the building's, and energy use. It is usually much more than your capital outlay.

> ### *Standard method of lifecycle costing*
> The BS ISO (BSI Group, 2008) method of lifecycle costing produces consistent and robust reports and will reveal lifetime savings as a consequence of sustainable interventions.

Promoting sustainable buildings

Financial incentives

Direct incentives for sustainable building design have evolved to serve government policies. These are listed by the Department of Energy and Climate Change (DECC) and have included:

- **The Green Deal:** opportunities to get a capital loan to carry out sustainable improvements to existing houses, paying it back as you save energy beginning in 2012.
- **Feed-in Tariffs (FITs):** financial opportunities to sell surplus energy generated locally back to the grid.
- **Renewable Heat Incentives:** financial incentives for the installation of renewable heating systems beginning in spring 2011.
- **Grants, council tax deductions, and subsidy programmes, such as Warm Front**, to encourage the installation of energy-efficient appliances.
- continuing grants available from your Local Authority, Defra, or organisations such as the Carbon Trust.

Broad government targets

Both the UK government and the European Union (EU) are focused on mitigating climate change, with controls on carbon emissions becoming more stringent over time. There are now obligations on energy suppliers, building clients and owners framed to help meet the overall objectives of the government.

In March 2007 the EU agreed to adopt the European Renewable Energy Directive, which commits Europe to providing 20% of the energy consumed from renewable sources by 2020.

The UK current Carbon Reduction Commitment (CRC) is to reduce CO_2 emissions to 80% of 1990 levels by 2050.

The Carbon Reduction Commitment

The Carbon Reduction Commitment Energy Efficiency Scheme (CRC) is very relevant to clients of large organisations but not smaller ones. In force since April 2010, the CRC aims to significantly reduce UK carbon emissions not covered by other pieces of legislation, the primary focus being to reduce emissions in non-energy intensive sectors in the UK. This complements the role of climate change agreements and the EU emissions trading scheme, which are directed primarily at energy-intensive organisations.

It is a mandatory scheme to cover all organisations using more than 6000 MWh per year of electricity (equivalent to an annual electricity bill of about £500,000) or with a half-hour tariff meter fitted. A ceiling for carbon emissions set for each organisation must be met by efficiency or by trading carbon credits.

Legal requirements

The legislative context changes constantly and in the end it is your responsibility to see that your project complies with the law. Failure to meet the legislative targets associated with your project may add to your costs in the form of fines or requirement to carry out remedial work.

There are many legal instruments that govern what you can design and build. They not only ensure the health and safety of the users but are also for the benefit of the wider community. These controls extend to supporting sustainable design. For example, they cover:

- insulation levels to reduce energy consumption
- energy sources to reduce CO_2 emissions
- use of water resources
- flood control management
- use of materials with respect to toxicity
- waste and pollution management during and after construction
- costs of waste disposal to landfill
- protection of biodiversity and the natural environment.

The design professionals on your team will be familiar with the relevant laws and regulations and will help you to comply throughout the project. Often there are benefits in going beyond mere compliance.

Mandatory requirements

Building Regulations

Organised into parts, the Building Regulations impose minimum standards of energy efficiency for new buildings and for existing buildings when they are altered or extended.

Part L, Conservation of fuel and power, is aimed at reducing GHG emissions from energy use in buildings, and to adapt building practice to the consequences of climate change. The 2010 edition of Part L1 is designed to reduce energy use in new dwellings by 25% (relative to 2006 standards) and, if planned changes go ahead, by 40% from 2013. New dwellings and publicly-owned buildings (including schools and colleges) will be expected to be zero carbon by 2016, and other new non-domestic buildings by 2019 (see Figure 2).

The current Part L requires a coordinated design approach which includes determining a servicing strategy and working towards an appropriate energy performance certificate from the start.

Other sections of the Building Regulations with direct relevance to sustainability are Part D (Toxic substances), Part F (Ventilation) and Part G (Sanitation, hot water safety and water efficiency).

The government's planning portal[3] gives a wide range of information about the building regulations and other legislative requirements related to building construction.

Code for Sustainable Homes

Exclusively for new domestic buildings, the Code for Sustainable Homes sets broad environmental performance standards covering energy and CO_2 emissions, water, materials, surface water run-off, waste, pollution, health and well-being, management and ecology.

Ratings are measured in six levels, which include specific targets for energy performance and water usage together with tradable targets for other aspects of sustainability. On energy, the requirements are a percentage reduction in carbon emissions compared with Building Regulations Part L1 (2006).

---

3   www.planningportal.gov.uk/buildingregulations

	2010	2013	2016	2019
What Part L proposes	30 kg CO_2/m^2/year	21 kg CO_2/m^2/year	8 kg CO_2/m^2/year	Carbon neutral
	DEC C rating	DEC B rating	DEC A rating	DEC A+ rating
	Use natural ventilation where possible	Relax warm-weather dress code	Relax dress code to allow thermal adaptive comfort	Test building design to UKCIP 2080
	Provide external shading and internal blinds	Thermal mass in roof, and add low-grade cooling to natural ventilation	Natural ventilation with comfort cooling or mechanical ventilation with heat recovery	Add insulated shutters/blinds with reflective outer coating
What you can do	2% average daylight factor	Use narrow plan floorplate or rooflights for daylighting (>2% average daylight factor)	Automatic adjustable external shading Consider deciduous planting Design according to daylighting (>3% average)	80% of floorplate daylight factor >5% average, with reflection onto vertical surfaces
	Encourage users to switch off PCs nightly	Consider laptop use, install kill switch for non-essentials	Lower power terminals with centralised computing	Add LEDs and new lighting technologies Use off-site internet-based cloud-computing systems

Figure 2: Proposed upgrades to Part L regulations between 2013–19 will establish more stringent energy criteria for new buildings. Source: adapted from Max Fordham Consulting Engineers, in association with *The Architect's Journal*, 1 May to 30 September 2010, Decoding Sustainability series, *The Architect's Journal*, London.

The highest level is 6, rated as zero carbon, which means that over the year the net amount of carbon produced from all energy use in the home is zero. All new publicly funded housing must achieve a level 3 but the government is about to introduce a local standards framework which may mean there will be varying standards applied to public and private housing. Aiming higher will have future advantages and some designers and clients are already aiming for levels 4–6. (The code, which is not written for clients, nonetheless contains information that might interest you. It may be downloaded from www. planningportal.gov.uk.)

Consideration is being given to making it mandatory to assess all new housing using the code, although particular levels have not yet been made mandatory nationally.

Energy Performance Certificates

Public authorities are now obliged to demonstrate their building's energy performance. The Energy Performance of Buildings Directive (EPBD), which came into force in Europe in January 2003, requires the occupiers of public buildings to display a Display Energy Certificate (DEC). This shows how energy efficient the building is on the basis of measured energy use over time in relation to the area of the building. On a standard scale of A–G, certificates show much CO_2 is released. 'A' represents the best level and is currently rarely achieved. 'G' is the lowest level. On average, older buildings are likely to be relatively less energy efficient than new ones and a typical public building is currently likely to achieve 'D' or 'E'.

For newly constructed or newly tenanted non-public buildings, an Energy Performance Certificate (EPC) is required showing designed energy efficiency using the same scale. Because actual performance is not measured, many buildings therefore achieve a higher rating, typically between 'B' and 'C'. These certificates do not need to be publicly displayed. It is likely that, in future, these certificates will be modified to include the embodied carbon of the materials used in new construction in the scale.

Embodied energy or embodied carbon

This is the name for the total energy or carbon emissions involved in acquiring (e.g. digging up minerals, cutting down trees), processing (e.g. smelting iron and forming steel, making window frames), and delivering the materials used to construct the building. Not yet a precise science, standards for calculating this are nonetheless being developed.

As buildings become more energy efficient to meet new regulations, the relative impact of embodied energy increases. Reliable ways of accounting for it will become increasingly important over time.

Environmental Impact Assessment

A number of European Directives require you to undertake environmental impact assessments (EIAs). Your design team is normally obliged to prepare an EIA that describes the ways in which the building complies with appropriate legislation as a condition of achieving planning consent. It should cover the full range of issues, not only energy but including all environmental topics such as preserving local biodiversity.

The local agenda

There are some prescriptive documents at a national level, such as Planning Policy Statements (PPSs), which shape local plans and drive government policy requirements, such as PPS 1 on Delivering sustainable development or PPS 22 on Renewable energy. As well as these national targets, individual local authorities may set their own additional targets. An example is the so-called 'Merton Rule', developed in the London Borough of Merton in 2003 (and adopted by many local authorities). The government is consulting on a new National Planning Policy Framework which may change the PPSs from their current form.

Other targets

There are other targets advocated by voluntary or private organisations that might be relevant, depending on your project. Your design team will be able to say which apply. Some are required by funders, including the government, even when they are not part of general legislation. The more important ones are described below.

BREEAM

The Building Research Establishment Energy Assessment Method (BREEAM) tool is available tailored to different building types. Long established, it has gradually been extended to embrace more than energy. It covers management of the project, health and well-being, energy, transport, water, materials, waste, land use and efficiency, pollution and innovation. Government funding might depend on achieving a high BREEAM rating. You can aspire to the highest ratings – such as 'Very good' or 'Outstanding', though lower ones also cover the wide range of the issues involved in sustainable design. The BREEAM website (www.breeam.org) contains links to useful references and material.

AECB standards

The Association for Environment Conscious Building (AECB) is an association for organisations and individuals interested in supporting and leading the drive for sustainable buildings. Although not an accreditation body, it publishes guidance on good practice and standards.[4] For example, its water standards prioritise reductions in environmentally damaging water use, targeting hot water use and water use in times and places of drought stress.

To avert the very real risk of building users retrofitting inefficient appliances, the standards specify performance and solutions that work in the real world. The AECB's CarbonLite programme is a step-by-step guide for creating and using low-energy buildings with low CO_2 emissions, aimed at clients, developers, design teams, builders and building users. It fills the gap between the aspiration to deliver high-performance buildings and the often more disappointing reality.

---

4   www.aecb.net/standards_and_guidance.php

PassivHaus

PassivHaus[5] (literally, 'passive house' in German) refers to a specific construction standard resulting in excellent comfort conditions achieved using low-energy or passive technologies. The principles can be applied to commercial, industrial and public building as well as houses. The technique uses high levels of insulation, minimal thermal bridges, excellent airtightness, well thought-out use of solar and internal heat gains, efficient components, a whole building ventilation system and heat recovery, to achieve exceptionally low running costs. To meet the PassivHaus standard requires:

- the total energy demand for space heating and cooling is less than 15 $kWh/m^2/$ year of treated floor area, compared to a UK national average of 140 $kWh/m^2/year$
- the total primary energy use for all appliances, domestic hot water and space heating and cooling is less than 120 $kWh/m^2/year$, compared to a UK national average of roughly 280 $kWh/m^2/year$.

These figures are verified at the design stage using the PassivHaus planning package. To maintain the design intent requires rigorous on-site quality control of workmanship, particularly to achieve the desired airtightness and thermal insulation.

Zero carbon

The definition of the 'zero carbon' concept is open to interpretation.[6] It is usually thought of as applying to buildings which generate as much renewable energy on-site as they consume – both for heating/cooling and lighting and internal appliances. The ambition is that all new homes will be zero carbon by 2016.

For buildings run by organisations covered by the CRC emissions scheme, the concept of zero carbon also extends to the idea of carbon credits.[7] These organisations receive an allotment of credits, called a cap. If they 'spend' more than this cap, they have to buy more credits at great financial cost, thus giving them an incentive to reduce emissions.

Soft Landings

A sustainable building will only perform as well as the occupier who uses it. You will need a 'user manual' to explain how your building works. However, without planning, forethought and adequate communication, the 'user manual' can easily be neglected,

---

5   www.passivhaus.org.uk
6   www.zerocarbonhub.org/definition.aspx
7   www.carbontrust.co.uk/policy-legislation/business-public-sector/pages/carbon-reduction-commitment.aspx

with detrimental consequences. To that end, the RIBA recommends a 'Soft Landings' approach (see text box) enshrined in the following principles:

- **Plan how your building will be managed and maintained from the start.** Management and maintenance plans that allow people easily to use your building sustainably should feature in your brief.
- **Review and sign off designs in reference to your brief.** Satisfy yourself that the concept design and, later, the detailed design meet your sustainable criteria and will be fit for purpose, straightforward to maintain, future-proof against changes in use, and ultimately easy to recycle at the end of the building's life.
- **From the start, plan to monitor the sustainable performance of your building after completion.** Keeping in touch with your design team will allow you to check that your building delivers the planned sustainable benefits.
- **Arrange regular reviews of your building and its systems.** During the first year and from time to time thereafter, carry out checks to make sure that everything is performing optimally. This is especially relevant if you plan to undertake another project, allowing you to learn valuable lessons.

Soft Landings

Recommended to architects by the RIBA, a 'Soft Landings' approach is a way to ensure that the building in use meets your design aspirations. It is the name for a framework overseen by a charitable organisation called the Usable Buildings Trust to help people to carry out construction projects in the spirit described here. It expects extended duties from the design and construction team:

- at inception and briefing stage to ensure effective dialogue between designer, contractor, client, end-user and building manager
- during design to review how the building will work from the occupier's point of view and manage expectations
- preparing for handover
- aftercare for 4–6 weeks following handover
- extended aftercare, monitoring and feedback for the first 3 years of use, so that the building operates as the design intended and shared learning can be embedded in future projects.

Regardless of the type of project, the concept of Soft Landings is a way to ensure that the intentions of the project are carried through into the design, commissioning and use of the building.

Sustainability adds value for you

As well as being good for environmental reasons, there are additional benefits in exceeding current minimum legislative targets. These include:

- **Reduced operating cost.** The primary benefit, increasingly important as energy costs rise.
- **Increased value.** Because of the lower running costs and the other benefits, sustainable buildings are more attractive to purchasers, which improves their resale or rental values. This matters to a single homeowner as much as to a large corporation. Research by the Royal Institute of Chartered Surveyors (RICS) shows that energy-efficient buildings attract higher prices in the market (RICS, 2009). This research is being supplemented by further work by BRE Global, RICS and the Investment Property Databank.
- **Future-proofing.** Building to higher standards future-proofs it against increases in standards as legislation tightens requirements.
- **Positive public relations.** If you are a business client, occupying a sustainable building will bolster your organisation's reputation or brand image.
- **Generating excess energy.** For example, to power your electric car or even your car fleet.

There are things you can do to embed sustainability at different stages:

Concept
- Test options to achieve your goals to see whether you actually need a building project.
- Write a statement of your vision and goals for sustainability and ensure that everyone buys into it.
- Show leadership. Communicate your vision to your team throughout the project.
- If there are others such as funders and senior board members involved in your project, canvass them to make them aware of the economic case for a sustainable building.

Setting targets

- Review the energy costs of your existing building with the help of cost consultants or your client advisor.
- Work out targets for reducing energy costs – especially by cutting down energy inputs as far as possible.
- With the help of your design team, decide if you can set your targets above the minimum requirements for longer term benefits.
- Ask your advisors about the relevant government incentives and grants.
- Carry out a strategic cost-benefit analysis to review the benefits and value of a sustainable project and incorporate your conclusions into your business case.
- Develop your criteria for sustainability success. Consider things such as annual carbon use, waste and recycling during construction and use, occupant comfort, food miles for catering services, and so on.

Preparation for action

- Establish ways to monitor performance. For example, undertake regular checks, surveys, zoned metering and visible displays indicating energy use.
- Familiarise yourself with the legislative context and satisfy yourself that your team members are up to date.
- Write a strategic brief, stating the general sustainability targets you wish to incorporate, e.g. BREEAM or Code for Sustainable Homes level, with help of specialist advice.

Part 2

The client's role in the building project

As the client for a project you have a key role. Your aspirations and vision should drive the project. It is your brief and your building. Your level of control during the project, for example in selecting designers, choosing construction approaches or deciding finishes, is in part determined by how it is delivered – that is by the procurement process. For example, using a traditional contract gives you more control and higher financial risks; design and build gives greater cost certainty but removes some of your control. Nonetheless in all projects you can provide leadership and ensure that you agree the directions that the project is taking. It is important always to ask for explanations of the impact of major decisions on long-term sustainability.

A commitment to sustainability must permeate the entire project if it is to be effectively achieved and there are some general 'rules' for you to use that will influence decisions in the right direction.

Client actions | *Embedding sustainability starting at the earliest stage*

1. Decide what you want to achieve in terms of sustainability. State your position clearly from the outset so that everyone involved understands and 'buys into' a sustainable approach.
2. State clearly your vision and goals for the project, taking your sustainability ambitions, including your intention to reduce lifetime costs, into account.
3. Review the energy costs of your existing building with the help of cost consultants or your client advisor and consider how to reduce this – especially by cutting down energy inputs as far as possible.
4. Test options to achieve your goals to see whether you actually need a building project.
5. Start a strategic cost-benefit analysis to review the benefits and value of a sustainable project and incorporate these into your business case.
6. Develop your criteria for sustainability success. Consider things such as annual carbon use, waste and recycling during construction and use, occupant comfort, food miles for your catering services.

7. Establish ways to monitor performance using, for example, regular checks, surveys, zoned metering and visible displays indicating energy use.
8. Communicate enough to be sure that your team is aligned with your vision throughout.
9. Canvas others involved, such as funders and senior board members, and make them aware of the economic case for a sustainable building.
10. Find out about incentives and grants that may apply to your situation.
11. Start to familiarise yourself with the legislative context to assure yourself that your team members are up to date.
12. Decide if you can set your targets above the minimum requirements, for longer term benefits.
13. Create or agree a statement of need and a strategic brief, stating the general sustainability targets you wish to incorporate, e.g. BREEAM, Code for Sustainable Homes level, etc., with help of specialist advice if needed.

Team collaboration during and after the project

It cannot be emphasised enough how much a successful building project depends on collaboration between you – the owner and/or user – and your team of designers and constructors. Shared knowledge and expertise of all team members, including you, in a holistic approach is the key. This includes a commitment from your team to communicate progress iteratively using a Soft Landings approach (see page 23).

Get things right at the start

As with all complex projects, your early decisions are the most important. For example, those about location, orientation and scale are irrevocable. Others, such as how to construct and service the building, get progressively more difficult and expensive to change over time. Resist the temptation to rush into it (see Figure 3).

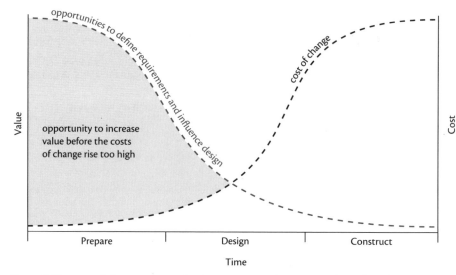

Figure 3: The cost of changes to a project increases over time. Source: CABE (2003).

Client design advisors

The Office of Government Commerce (OGC) recommends for large projects that you appoint an independent client advisor at the start of your project, even before you appoint a project manager. They will be able to assess what is possible for your project, help you to develop the business case and procurement strategy, and will review designs for their affordability and quality.

The RIBA maintains a register of accredited RIBA Client Design Advisors (CDAs). CDAs are usually architects (but not the ones designing the building) sitting on the client's side of a project, independent of the supply team, monitoring and helping to manage the design process from its earliest stages. CDAs are selected from the RIBA's international membership for their all-round procurement expertise, design experience, business knowledge and track-record of delivering results in construction projects.

For the best outcome, the client should at all times:

- Ensure that aspirations of all stakeholders are aligned and that they are kept informed.

- Consider location and transport issues as part of the building project decisions; the journey to work and delivery miles can be large sources of CO_2 emissions and contribute to the carbon footprint.
- Understand the user role beyond the design decisions phase: managers and users are key to meeting design targets. Try to have users represented from the start as part of the 'client', demand-side, team even if they are not part of your organisation.
- Keep it simple: complex buildings and control systems are harder for users to manage and often perform much less well than design predictions.
- Seek expert advice and ask as many questions as you need to – it is your building. Organisations such as the BRE, the PassivHaus Trust, Usable Buildings Trust or AECB as well as your design team, can offer advice about standards, accreditation or grants as well as about design principles.

Whatever the procurement process, goals must be fully communicated as control passes from one part of the team to another, or a 'gap' can occur through which the sustainable design intentions can disappear and get lost. A process such as Soft Landings to help follow through sustainable concepts must be built in or results are less likely to meet expectations. As Soft Landings incorporates a commitment to monitor performance in use this affects both the team interactions and the actual design and needs to be factored in as early as possible.

The OGC uses a 'Gateway' process to help clients guide projects of many kinds, identifying review and decision points at 'gateways' 0–5, from the earliest business justification to the ready for use and post-project evaluations stages. The RIBA has an 'Outline Plan of Work' covering activities of design professionals in stages A–L from assessing need, through briefing, design and construction stages to evaluation of the final building. The appendix, 'What to do when', aligns client actions that are suggested throughout this document with these process 'route maps' to illustrate how they fit to the sequence of decisions that are made throughout the project. Figure 5 in the appendix indicates an approximation of when the client actions listed here may need to take place, though different project structures may change this timing.

Once you embark on a building project, you need to think about user behaviour and management of the finished buildings, which affect initial decisions and likely effectiveness of proposed solutions. These themes reappear throughout the discussion that follows.

Client actions | *As the project begins*

14. Take advice about procurement options noting the varied extent of direct relationship with the design team in the different ways of delivering a building project.

15. Set up a Soft Landings approach and identify who is responsible for coordinating the sustainability impact of decisions and the programme for monitoring the building in use.
16. Whatever procurement approach is used, give your time to communication – it is your views that count.
17. Look at location options bearing in mind travel for staff, users, visitors and deliveries over the life of the building.
18. Review options for keeping the size of proposed space to a minimum with appropriate flexibility to adapt to future change.
19. Start planning how the completed building will be managed and what information will be needed.
20. Select a design or integrated delivery team using advisors to help if necessary. Focus on skill levels and attitudes of designers in relation to sustainable agenda and review candidates carefully.

Client actions | *As the project progresses*

21. Have regular meetings or updates to keep yourself, as well as your organisation, users and relevant local groups informed and involved. As the project progresses they may make valuable inputs.
22. Have a plan to keep continuity and sustain your vision if team members and individuals change.
23. Review your strategic brief and the sustainability targets you have set, and seek cost-benefit advice about aiming as high as possible.
24. Then review the detailed design brief including how sustainability targets are being developed and will be met. Sign off these targets as well as the accommodation schedule.
25. Once the concept design is developed, check that it addresses your brief, and later the detailed design, before signing them off.
26. When the concept design is agreed, start to review issues related to management of the finished building with user representatives and your designers.
27. As a construction approach is determined and materials begin to be selected prior to planning application, verify with your design team how sustainability is being ensured and whether embodied energy of materials is being considered.
28. As the design progresses, request information about what environmental performance is being predicted by models.

Evaluating your team

Your team, in-house as well as professional consultants, makes a big difference to the outcome. Its selection is an important moment in the project process. You need to investigate team members' track records, examine what they have achieved, gauge how well they understand your aspirations and assess how well they will be able to work together. Various forms of competitive selection are available. There is client guidance on the RIBA website and if a competitive selection is adopted the RIBA competitions department can help with advice and management.

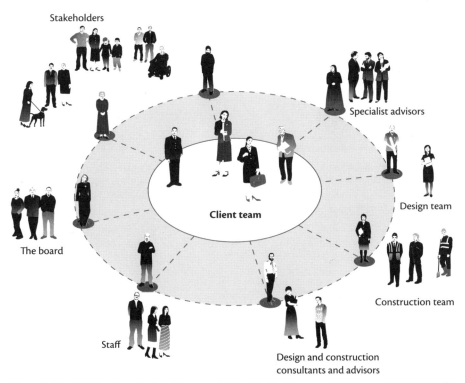

Figure 4: The client and professional teams relationships for large projects. Source: CABE (2003).

While it is reasonable to expect your design team to know how to work towards achieving your brief, you will sometimes want to ask questions at appropriate moments to satisfy yourself that your building will really serve you well and meet your aspirations. Some or all of the following may be useful when selecting designers and specialists:

- Find out about the commitment and knowledge of the whole team – do they view sustainability in a comprehensive way? – you can ask:
  - What is their attitude to targets (e.g. does low or zero carbon for them mean designing for minimum energy requirements first and considering other efficiency measures after that to provide for long-term energy efficiency, or do they rely on adding sophisticated equipment to control carbon emissions – which implies a failure to design on energy-efficient principles)?
  - What relevant issues other than energy efficiency do they include in their approach to sustainability, e.g. water conservation, minimising construction wastes, user comfort, others?
  - What is their track record of building sustainably? What accreditation have they achieved in other projects – BREEAM, other?
  - Have there been post-occupancy evaluations that have measured specific elements like real energy and water use, user comfort, that confirm that they are meeting the initial targets?
  - Are they used to working in a multi-skilled way with many disciplines? Do they use the advice of 'green' engineers, ecologists or other sustainability specialists where relevant?
  - Do they use baseline projections for design (page 12) to decide on requirements for existing climate change effects?
- See them at work together in their office or at interview. How people lead a team and motivate good performance from all, affects the outcome.
- Ask about the services engineering consultants and the individuals in their teams and how they work with architects. If teams have worked together before this is a good sign though not essential. They do, however, need to respect and understand each other's work.

Important considerations for a sustainable project

The four topics discussed below are energy (including embodied energy), water, waste and pollution and user health and well-being. These topics reflect the structure of energy assessment methods, for example BREEAM, and tend to be handled separately in legislation, although they interact and overlap and must, therefore, also be considered as a whole.

Some decisions are ones in which the client – the demand side – plays a key role, others are for the supply side – the design team – to take a lead. To some degree these all involve collaboration between the client and an expert team who will start by developing your initial strategic brief into a detailed design brief.

Energy: opportunities for an efficient project

Opportunities for saving energy and minimising carbon emissions arise in almost every aspect of new and refurbishment projects:

- the design process
- the construction process
- the materials used
- the amount of energy such as heating, cooling or lighting needed to run the building over its life
- the amount of energy such as power to workplace equipment or catering used by occupants for their activities
- how efficiently this energy is provided
- how the building is accessed and used by its users.

Minimising initial energy requirements is an important starting point. Using renewable energy sources and locally generated energy is an additional way of reducing carbon emissions.

Half the demand $\times$ twice the efficiency $=$ quarter of the CO_2

Most design decisions have an influence on energy requirements. Some of the early ones need your input, such as location and building size, and they have a major impact on what can be achieved in the design. Others may be largely decided by the design team. The depth of a building from side to side affects how natural ventilation can work for cooling and air quality. The ceiling height and window pattern affect the use that can be made of daylight and options for external sun-screening. The design team has to balance its design ideas in these and all other matters with your needs, funds and circumstances to achieve your goals.

Some of the most important topics are covered below with an indication of who plays the major role in decisions.

Location

Client decision. Location should be considered early as part of initial option appraisals and be revisited at the start of the building project.

Where is your site? Travel patterns for users, both staff and visitors, and movement of goods, have a major bearing on the energy use attributable to a building. You should consider this even for refurbishment projects. Inefficient locations should be the first that you phase out or put to uses better suited to the location. It is an essential part of the long-term equation for new projects and you need to consider it prominently in option appraisals prior to a commitment to invest.

Size

Client decision. Size should be considered in initial option appraisals and be revisited at the start of the building project.

The correct amount of space for the desired functions is equally important. A building that is too large uses unnecessary energy. Space per person matters and you need to consider not only area per occupant but also how frequently people will be there – space utilisation patterns. If virtual interaction, using a telephone, video link or newer technologies such as Skype or social networking tools, is an option it can reduce the overall space requirement and provide user benefits from minimising travel time.

How the building is managed once occupied will have the greatest effect on these concepts, but they need to be discussed and understood at the design stage to avoid over-sizing the building and to enable potential changes in future use patterns to be tested and allowed for.

Building management

Client decision but discuss with design team. Once the building is under construction there is an opportunity to create manuals and user information packs to assist effective behaviour management.

Will you be managing your building? If not make sure your assumptions about how it will be used are communicated to the occupier through manuals and user information. Management is often ignored at the design stage, but is vital to energy saving. The targets for comfort that are set in the brief, the ease with which users can control heat, light and air, methods to monitor, and perhaps modify, energy use all impact on the lifetime cost to you or the occupier. Design decisions need to consider user behaviour so that fittings, layouts and management options help users to be energy efficient. For example, zoned metering can be 'smart' with information displays which help users save energy by understanding where waste occurs in unoccupied areas/times and adjust systems to work better. You can include facilities management skills on your team initially to help incorporate design concepts early on that will encourage responsible user behaviour.

Some relevant questions to discuss from the start of the project include:

- Who is developing policies or explanation/training for behaviour in use and are they represented in the design team discussions?
- Have user representatives had input to waste and recycling locations, information technology use assumptions, cleaning regime requirements and other activities relevant to a building in use?
- What scenarios for future functional changes have been explored and what will that imply for demolition/rebuilding?
- Will feedback on energy use and water consumption be visible, easily understood in relation to what people are doing and thus able to help them manage their behaviour?
- Has a review been planned (a post-occupancy evaluation) looking at how the building performs once occupied, so that the project provides an ongoing learning environment for you and your team?

Flexibility/adaptability

Joint decision by client and design team.

Spaces need to be multifunctional wherever possible so that they do not sit empty for large proportions of the time. For example, schools are increasingly being used during the evenings and weekends by members of their local community. This is something that can be addressed throughout the life of a building even when very minor refurbishments are being carried out. Flexibility also concerns the ability to make changes to the building without destroying and disposing of too much of the existing building. Adapting a space or group of spaces with minimum waste will in itself reduce energy use over the life of the building, as well as containing cost in use. This relates to the importance of being able to demount and reuse all the building components as they come to the end of their life. Adaptability should take into account the lifecycle of different parts of the building which varies: furniture arrangements change frequently, partitions every 5 years or so, services every 12–15 years and structural elements much less often or never.

External conditions

Designers' decisions are usually set rather early – you may wish to have the implications explained.

Managing the impact of the external conditions is the first stage of energy efficiency. Using high levels of insulation, shading from heat gain, good night cooling and low-energy fittings help to achieve a high level of comfort for users with minimum use of energy or mechanical intervention. Building orientation, and the opportunities offered by each specific site in relation to local climate conditions such as sun and shade, rain and wind, soil and plant, for example, are highly significant and in some, though not all, situations offer great opportunities. If a fully 'passive' approach is being adopted detailed information about the site and its micro-climate is fundamental, but for all projects the site is always relevant and important to achieve energy efficiency as well as other benefits.

Renewable energy locally sourced

A design team decision.

Renewable non-carbon-based energy sources or locally produced energy may be considered. This must not be 'bolt on' just for current tax reasons or to exploit the opportunities to sell energy back to the grid, or in order to gain a 'green' reputation. Your design team needs to assess what would work in your situation and advise you how they could integrate renewable energy with their overall servicing and energy conservation strategy. The merits of the different approaches for your location should be explored using an options appraisal method. There are many possible options such as heat pumps, combined heat and power or solar thermal heating but these must be carefully matched to the project and are never as effective as reducing the overall demand for energy.

Construction materials and finishes

A design team decision.

The embodied energy of construction materials is one aspect of the energy equation to be considered. Low embodied energy is desirable from the climate change mitigation perspective and is especially important in short-life buildings. Although currently there are only a few direct incentives – such as the need to achieve a specific rating in BREEAM – to use materials with low embodied energy, these may often be cheaper in real terms and are likely to be favoured as energy costs rise.

The embodied energy of a really well-insulated building, with limited user activity, such as a storage warehouse, can be as much as 60% of its lifetime energy use, showing how important this aspect may be. Even in more usual situations where energy use for occupant comfort is a significant factor, the embodied energy in the materials from which it is made could amount to 20% over its life, according to the Recovery Insulation Project, a figure well worth reducing by care in choice of materials.

Embodied energy is low when material is:

- produced and processed locally so that energy used in transport is low
- robust so that it has a long life
- able to be easily replaced when it wears out by equally energy efficient, sustainable items
- able to be easily reused or recycled after building demolition thereby reducing the embodied energy of its next use.

Reusing building materials can sometimes save nearly 95% of otherwise wasted embodied energy. Responsible sourcing of materials considers not only embodied energy but also asks:

- Was it from a renewable source, e.g. timber from sustainably managed forests?
- Was it from a responsibly managed source including where production helps disadvantaged populations?
- Is it finished with non-toxic finishes?
- Is it cleanable using eco-friendly (biodegradable) materials?
- Is it not contributing to ozone layer depletion?

Water: efficient resource management

Designing responsibly in relation to water involves the site, the systems and fittings installed in the building and user behaviour. The design team must be prepared to answer questions relating to these issues – how far have they all been considered? Which can be incorporated? What training do users need?

The site

Design decisions but they often result in prominent external features so client input in relation to image is important.

Impermeable external surfaces are more and more widely used, preventing the soil from absorbing rainfall so it is necessary to plan how to absorb rain and flash floods into surrounding landscape. The site offers major opportunities to avoid problems and gain benefits from water. The design can control and manage rainfall whether onto the ground or a roof.

Rainwater can be collected for use in systems that do not need treated water, such as WCs and plant watering. Water can be collected on the site to act as a feature externally, to absorb heavy rainfall and flood water, to make use of evaporative cooling, and to irrigate local shade plants. 'Green' planted roofs, particularly sedum roofs, allow plants to benefit from rainfall and protect the building, and enable the roof to contain water for a while and slow its passage to the ground reducing flood risks.

Sustainable drainage systems: SUDS

SUDS consist of structures to manage surface water run-off. They are used to prevent flooding and pollution. There are four general methods of control:

- filter strips and swales
- permeable surfaces and filter drains
- infiltration devices
- basins and ponds.

These controls should be located to where they can best control the rate of run-off. They also provide different levels of treatment for surface water, using the natural processes of sedimentation, filtration, adsorption and biological degradation. They are suitable for most hard and soft built-up sites.

The Construction Industry Research Association (CIRIA) website provides information about the Interim Code of Practice for SUDS prepared by the National SUDS working group.[8]

Systems and fittings

Design decisions.

Sanitary fittings that use less water have long been available and are now often a requirement. Appropriately sized gutters and rainwater management systems as well as suitable roof designs may be needed to cope with the impact of heavy storms.

---

8   www.ciria.org.uk/suds/icop.htm

User behaviour

Client decisions about management.

User behaviour has a major impact on water use. Running taps, failure to exploit low-flush options, poor maintenance and leaks – all of these waste water. Making water suitable to drink is very energy intensive, contributing 0.5% to the UK's GHG emissions. The water industry estimates that 2–3% of all electricity used in the UK goes to making waste water drinkable. Water meters may in future provide a feedback monitoring system, as with energy use, which will make it easier for users to see when their behaviour is acting contrary to the intentions of the building. An increasing population with higher standards of comfort and cleanliness will make ever increasing demands on the available supply so wasting water is a serious issue.

Waste and pollution: reduction through management

The construction process

The cycle through building construction, operation and demolition uses resources (energy, water and materials) and creates waste at all stages. When any inputs or outputs can be reduced the whole cycle is more sustainable. Approximately one-third of overall UK waste arises from building construction and demolition activity on site. Of this, about 15% is wasted material that is delivered to site, paid for by you the client, but never used.

Contractors should not just be known for delivering a building to budget and on time. They should also have a good reputation and record for training staff to deliver quality in all details of site management as well as construction skills. The industry has become increasingly conscious of the profits associated with efficiency and waste reduction on site, and there are controls to enforce responsible behaviour. The BREEAM management credits cover the type of concerns that should be considered. WRAP[9] and SmartWASTE[10] have useful information.

Designing for health and well-being of users

Sustainable design affects users in many ways and it is important that this is understood and catered for by the design team. Comfort, good natural daylight, views, access to green spaces, well-located stairs encouraging people to walk rather than use lifts, protection from toxic and hazardous building materials and finishes are the type of things that have an effect on the health and well-being of building users.

---

9 www.wrap.org.uk/construction/index.html
10 www.smartwaste.co.uk

The questions below are not exhaustive, but are examples of what you can ask designers to ensure that you and they understand how their designs are dealing with issues of health and well-being.

Managing the impacts of external conditions:

- What percentage of the time could users accept failure to meet preferred temperatures? Five per cent of the time might be acceptable now; if carbon reduction targets mean that temperature levels cannot be so tightly controlled this is likely to rise.
- How is the desire for daylight being met? Careful interior planning can help make sure that daylight reaches appropriate locations.
- Are 'breathable' materials being considered to help control humidity? This is of increasing importance in a well-insulated airtight building. (Although this is not yet a regular concern, it will become an important issue as more airtight buildings are designed.)

Access to and views of outside spaces, especially if they are planted and contain trees, to reduce stress and/or provide for healthy exercise:

- What green space is available on site or planned in the local area?
- Healthy food and water: what provision is being made or is locally available?

Withstanding extremes:

- How are flood control, storm incidents, etc. being planned for and what speed of response do the building systems have to temperature extremes?
- Are specific external maintenance regimes needed to keep the building 'fit for purpose' in this respect, and where are they recorded?

Use of eco-friendly materials (e.g. treated with non-toxic finishes) and ones that can be cleaned using eco-friendly products (e.g. non-toxic and biodegradable) will avoid exposing users to unnecessary toxicity.

- How are cleaning needs being considered?
- How are cleaning regimes being recorded and communicated for future users?

Handover

Handover is when the building comes into your hands and starts its real life. What happens then is largely up to you – or the users occupying the building.

Keeping down waste and pollution

Everything that has been written so far requires that, for optimum effect, users understand how the building should 'work' in terms of energy and water use as well as cleaning requirements, maintenance and other features that have an impact on waste and pollution. There are many topics that might be relevant and they will vary for different types of building. The user in a housing development, for example, may be an autonomous householder wanting to know the energy use of particular household appliances, or see heating costs displayed near the thermostat. An organisation occupying a corporate office, or a head teacher of a school, may need more strategic information about the best way to manage temperature to accommodate variable occupancy in space and time, and how to get the message about not wasting water across to a wide user population. Users typically need regular reminding, incentives and help to behave in the way designers anticipated and need to be given agreed targets to meet.

A review of building operation after handover is an important part of getting the maximum benefit and value out of the building. It often takes a year or more for a building's energy systems to be fine-tuned to all the seasons, and to train operatives in their best use. A sustainable building is likely to need new user and building management skills and awareness for external features as well as internal systems. UK facilities managers may need extra help with unfamiliar features, such as green roofs, water evaporative ponds, ground source heat systems. Working with the design team, especially services engineers, to meet sustainability targets is important, particularly in the first few years, as they are most familiar with all the details of the systems and the management they have assumed will be in place. Once people have learned the best way to manage the systems, occasional reviews are adequate until systems come to be replaced.

Client actions | *As the construction finishes and the building comes into use*

29. Ensure that the monitoring process established initially (e.g. by using Soft Landings) is started as soon as services are turned on and tested.
30. Confirm the details of the process whereby the design and supply team keep in contact with you to help manage the building as it settles down.
31. Accept the building at handover with a clear and usable set of management information.
32. Plan refresher courses for users, regularly communicate incentives, to ensure the best possible user behaviour.
33. Arrange a programme of reviews in use, post-occupancy evaluations to take place regularly, starting when the building has been occupied for over 3 months.
34. Carry out regular comprehensive reviews of all the building systems to make sure they are performing optimally – this is important in the first year, useful for the first 3 years and needed from time to time thereafter.

Appendices

What to do when

As mentioned earlier, the decision process for a building project is iterative. Although these client actions, gathered from the document, have been aligned with the RIBA plan of work and the OGC gateway process, they may not all take place, may be repeated at different stages and may be relevant in a different order than that shown.

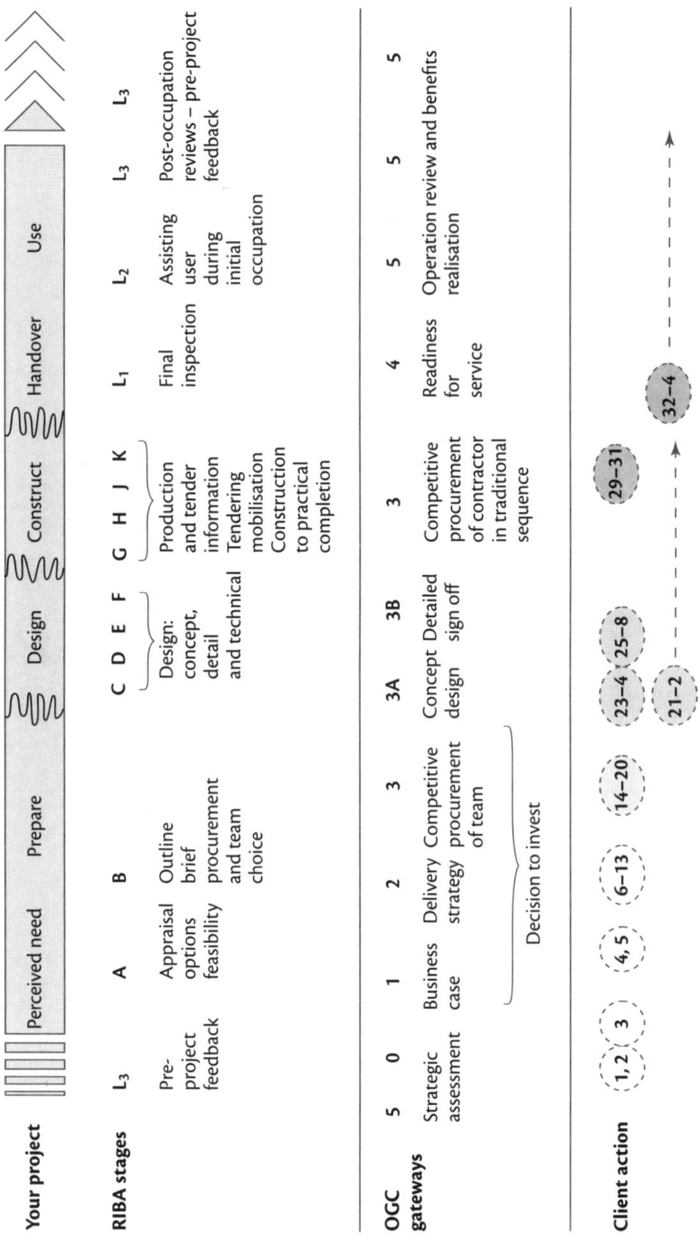

Your project	Perceived need	Prepare		Design	Construct	Handover	Use		
RIBA stages	L3	A	B	C D E F	G H J K	L1	L2	L3	L3
	Pre-project feedback	Appraisal options feasibility	Outline brief procurement and team choice	Design: concept, detail and technical	Production and tender information / Tendering mobilisation / Construction to practical completion	Final inspection	Assisting user during initial occupation	Operation review and benefits realisation	Post-occupation reviews – pre-project feedback
OGC gateways	5	0	1	2	3	3A	3B	3	4	5	5
	Strategic assessment		Business case	Delivery strategy	Competitive procurement of team	Concept design	Detailed sign off	Competitive procurement of contractor in traditional sequence	Readiness for service	Operation review and benefits realisation	Post-occupation reviews
				Decision to invest						
Client action	1, 2 3	4, 5	6–13	14–20	23–4	25–8		29–31	32–4		
					21–2						

Figure 5: Process route maps and client actions. Source: Alexi Marmot Associates.

Bibliography

References

Adams, W.M. (2006) The future of sustainability: re-thinking environment and development in the twenty-first century. *Report of the IUCN Renowned Thinkers Meeting*, 29–31 January 2006. http://cmsdata.iucn.org/downloads/iucn_future_of_sustanability.pdf.

Bruntland Report (1987) *Our Common Future*. Oxford University Press, Oxford.

BSI Group (2008). BS ISO 15686-5:2008, *Buildings and Constructed Assets. Service Life Planning. Life-cycle Costing*. BSI Group, London.

CABE (2003) *Creating Excellent Buildings: A Guide For Clients*. Commission for Architecture and the Built Environment, London.

Davis Langdon (2007) *Cost and Benefit of Achieving Green Buildings*. David Langdon, Australia. www.davislangdon.com/upload/StaticFiles/AUSNZ%20Publications/Info%20Data/InfoData_Green_Buildings.pdf.

Defra (2009) *Adapting to Climate Change: The UK Climate Projections* (UKCP09). Department for Environment, Food and Rural Affairs, London. http://ukclimateprojections.defra.gov.uk.

RICS (2009) *Doing Well By Doing Good? An Analysis of the Financial Performance of Green Office Buildings in the USA*. Royal Institution of Chartered Surveyors, London. www.rics.org/site/download_feed.aspx?fileID=5763&fileExtension=PDF.

Useful websites to explore

BRE PassivHaus UK: www.passivhaus.org.uk

BREEAM: www.breeam.co.uk

Building Regulations: www.planningportal.gov.uk/buildingregulations

Carbon Trust: www.carbontrust.co.uk

CIRIA – sustainable drainage systems: http://www.ciria.org/suds

Energy Saving Trust: www.energysavingtrust.org.uk

Environmental Association for Universities and Colleges: www.eauc.org.uk

Forest Stewardship Council: www.fsc-uk.org

Office of Government Commerce – Gateway process: www.ogc.gov.uk/what_is_ogc_gateway_review.asp

PassivHaus Trust: www.passivhaus.co.uk

RIBA: www.architecture.com

UK Green Building Council: www.ukgbc.org/site/resources

World Business Council for Sustainable Development: www.wbcsd.org

WRAP – Resource efficiency and recycled products and materials: www.wrap.org.uk/construction/index.html

Further reading

Dunster, B., Simmons, C. and Gilbert, B. (2007) *The ZEDBook*. Taylor & Francis, London.

Gething, B. (2010) *Design for Future Climate: Opportunities for Adaptation in the Built Environment*. Technology Strategy Board, Swindon.

Intergovernmental Panel on Climate Change (2007) *Assessment Report No. 4 Climate Change*. IPCC, Geneva.

International Passive House Association (2010) *The Passive House: Information for Property Developers, Contractors and Clients*. International Passive House Association, Darmstadt.

Kohler, N., Konig, H., Kressig, J. and Lutzkendorf, T. (2010) 'A life cycle approach to buildings'. *DETAIL Green*. Institut für internationale Architektur-Dokumentation, Munich.

Liddell, H. (2008) *Eco-minimalism: The Antidote to Eco-bling*. RIBA, London.

Mackay, D.J.C. (2009) *Sustainable Energy – Without the Hot Air*. UIT Cambridge, Cambridge.

McDonough, W. (2009) *Cradle to Cradle: Remaking the Way We Make Things*. Rodale Press, Emmaus, PA.

Roaf, S. (2004) *Closing the Loop: Benchmarks for Sustainable Buildings*. RIBA Publishing, London.

Royal Institute for British Architects (2009) *A Client's Guide to Engaging an Architect: Guidance for Hiring an Architect for your Project*. RIBA Publishing, London.

Stern, N. (2006) *The Economics of Climate Change: The Stern Review*. Cambridge University Press, Cambridge.

Vale, R. and Vale, B. (2002) *The New Autonomous House: Designing and Planning for Sustainability*. Thames & Hudson, London.